3 Warnings

Excerpted from

*Kafka's Roach
The Life and Times of
Gregor Samsa*

As Told by a Friend.

Marc Estrin

Copyright © 2017 Marc Estrin

ISBN: 978-1-944388-17-1

Fomite
Burlingon, VT
http://www.fomitepress.com

THREE WARNINGS
Excerpted from *Kafka's Roach*
The Life and Times of Gregor Samsa
As Told by a Friend.

Gregor Samsa, newly turned into a (six-foot, talking) cockroach, is planning a performance from his cage in a Viennese side show, a lecture on Spengler's Decline of the West. *The friend reminds the reader what the 1919 best-seller was all about.*

SPENGLER

He opens thus:

In this book is attempted for the first time the venture of forecasting history, of following the still untraveled stages in the destiny of a Culture, and specifically of the only Culture of our time and on our planet which is actually in the phase of fulfillment -- the West-European American.

"Forecasting history". What a bold assertion! History had heretofore concerned itself with the past. There were no Departments of Future Studies. Spengler was out there all alone. In order to forecast history, he had to discover, inductively, a grand pattern, an "inward form of History", repeating through all recorded time, and in every major culture -- and it was this:

For everything organic the notions of birth, death, youth, age, lifetime are fundamentals...

He saw all cultures he studied come into springlike being, youthful and vigorous, flower in their summery, unique ways, and then autumnally decay. Their winters were frozen into rigid, petrified forms, and these forms he called "civilization". Our Western culture had been born around the tenth century, flowered in the gothic and the Renaissance, became "civilized" in the eighteenth century, and in the nineteenth century, with the industrial revolution, had begun the process of spiritual decline. The upcoming death of Western Culture was as certain as that of any other living organism. History was Destiny, unfolded through the cycle of human cultures, all of which shared a common rhythm and pattern. We cannot choose our destiny, we cannot alter it. We have no choice but to make the best of our historical situation.

Stark. Dramatic. No wonder it attracted so much attention. In this wintertime essay, he drove his metaphor hard. When the freezing point of a culture is reached, like water, it expands and can shatter its container. Though spiritually exhausted, it gathers the technical and material capacity for outward reach, desperately grabbing at life. And so begins what he called an Age of Caesarism. He accurately predicted the coming of a totalitarian state, not by looking at the social movements around him, but by taking the longest possible view. He predicted a coming age of imperialist wars in which nations would complete their spiritual death, and finally fall to pieces, yes, like Rome, but also like every other culture, finally succumbing to the invasion of new forces, alien, hostile to the old, full of springlike, spontaneous creativity and religious devotion. In the inevitable final battle between civilized engineers and God-inspired barbarians, the engineers would go down clutching their pens and pencils. Artists would also succumb: this was not a time for soul. Art would be frustrated by society's rejection, or corrupted by its licentiousness and power -- a spiritual vocation gone astray. The Zeitgeist is inevitable, a time of perverted men in a hopelessly perverted age. Politics would consist of liars calling liars liars.

Gregor would be sure to emphasize this radical notion of "civilization". For us, the apogee of achievement, the targeted ideal, the goal toward which we stick and carrot benighted races. But for Spengler, the prelude to death and decay, with imperialism the typical symbol of the end.

At the time, G could hardly appreciate the uncanniness of Spengler's predictions. Writing as early as 1911, he had spoken of the endless repetition of the "already-accepted", of standardized art, of petrified formulas which would ignore and deny history. "Events," Spengler predicted, would become "the private affairs of the oligarchs and their assassins," and would arise from administration, not society. Even before the evidence of the war, he foresaw professional armies operating with an entirely different morality than civilian society. In 1917, he noted, "In a few years, we have learned to virtually ignore things which before the war would have petrified the world." Had he not died in '36, he might have seen more than even he could imagine.

Spengler clearly imagined "Generation X" and the couch-potato "End of History", the age of TINA (There Is No Alternative):

With the arrival of the Age of Empire there are no more political problems. People get along with the situation as it is and with the powers that be. In the age of the Embattled States, streams of blood reddened

3

the walls of world cities to transform the great truths of democracy into reality and achieve rights without which life did not seem worth living. Now these rights have been won, but not even punishment can move the grandchildren to make use of them....

This, in general. But there was one particular notion of Spengler's that intersected deeply with G's quest -- that of Faustian Man in a Faustian Culture. You'll forgive me for the non-inclusive language. It was Spengler's, and surely the language of the time. It was the term G used. Further, if one were to strive for strict accuracy, even "Faustian People" or "Faustian Humanity" would not cover G's participation. So let it be "Faustian Man", with appropriate apologies. By Spring of 1919, the term was well known to the German-speaking public, and the circus seminars could proceed without explanation. For us, now, it is not as obvious.

The contemporary person on the street, if asked to define the adjective "faustian", might, if he recognized it at all, refer to the "deal with the devil", the nature of Faust's bargain. But that was not Spengler's central thrust. Faustian culture, for him, was simply the latest of the three cultures which had inhabited and defined "the West".

The worldview of Classical culture, according to Spengler, (and his generalizations have caused him much grief), was centered in the statically present: its paradigmatic expression was plane geometry's eternal truths. Then, Magian culture, a term invented by Spengler, basically that of early Christianity, but (and this enraged the pigeonholers) also including Arabian and other Muslim cultures. Its primary image was the struggle between good and evil, light and darkness, God and the devil, creation and destruction. Its representative mathematics was the more dynamic algebra, variable qualities and quantities jostling each other in changing relation.

Our own Faustian culture, the latest condition of the West, is driven by tense striving toward aims and goals, each limited in themselves, but collectively pressing toward the infinite. Our history is an unfolding of that unchecked thrust. The whole course of Western mathematics can be seen as as "a long, secret, and finally victorious battle against the notion of magnitude", symbolized by the Faustian embrace of the infinitesimal calculus, the development of probability theory, and now, after Spengler's time, its universal application in quantum mechanics. Nothing less could satisfy the Faustian soul than deep, eternal simultaneous striving towards the infinitesimal and the infinite. Ever restless, ever longing for the unattainable. Endless vistas, limitless space. Faustian man, Faustian culture.

One could sense it early on in the upward thrust of the gothic cathedrals, their spires disappearing into the mist. One could follow it in the perspective studies of the Renaissance, the astounding capture of an infinite vanishing point on a two dimensional surface. Global exploration, abstract, "pure" music, machine after machine, driving, aspiring. The Reformation claiming the infinite capacity of individual souls.

Spengler develops his history with great lyric intensity. The Baroque striving for infinity, dissolving traditional forms into bewildering concatenations of curves and structural deceptions; painters like Caravaggio and Rembrandt pushing perspective and shadow to the farthest limits and metaphysical depths. The young movement for free inquiry and scientific speculation.

And then came autumn. The 18th century, according to Spengler, was the autumn of the Faustian soul, and there we find the last and most exquisite creations of its fully-realized forms. The infinity of Mozart, peering out in the finale of the G minor Symphony, out into interstellar 12-tone space. Kant, Goethe, the conclusive formulations of the deepest speculations of the age.

And finally winter, the "civilization" phase of the Faustian spirit. Our winter. Middle-class values reign, even among the ruling class. And thus the general formlessness, rejecting any standards of taste for a mindless, insouciant individualism, and a need for unrestricted freedom. Wide, meaningless fluctuations of style, and now the "post-modern" piling on of incongruous detail, no end of "experiments", life as life-style. Spengler predicted the inevitable end of masterpieces: the spiritual possibility of creating great paintings or music was simply exhausted.

Political forms, for Spengler, were similarly meaningless. The so-called democratic forms of parliaments and congresses were hollow masks obscuring the basic political reality -- the triumph of money. Everything was structured to yield to the power of financial speculation: constitutionalism, democracy, even socialism. Politicians of all stripes had no choice but to become paid agents of financiers. How Spengler would laugh at the current posturing around campaign finance reform, the emptiness of our rhetoric helplessly reflecting the inevitability of late Faustian dynamics.

His predictions were grim, as end-talk tends to be. They have, in their broad forms, come to pass. Before his death, Gregor Samsa encountered the most intense of them; we, his survivors, have also experienced the most pervasive.

THE THREE ISAIAHS

Gregor is working as the risk manager at the Manhattan Project in Los Alamos, New Mexico, where scientists are constructing the first atomic bombs. There has just been a Messiah performance.

But before the audience could conclude the event was over, Chaplain Capt. Jonathan Maple walked onstage, making his way through the departing chorus members, who were taking places at the back of the hall. Chaplain Maple was a gaunt thirty-five, with a high forehead under short black hair accentuating his skull-like visage, his somber eyes magnified by thick, round glasses. He had recently arrived on the mesa, a permanent replacement for the guest ministers, rabbis and priests whose coming-and-going Groves felt might compromise security. He had an office in the Big House, and was available by appointment for consultation. This, however, was his first general public appearance, and even those who might otherwise have fled stayed around to assess this new member of the community. I had mentioned Moll Flanders' two mistakes of the evening. This was the second.

Chaplain Maple began innocuously enough:

"I want to thank Dr. Flanders, Dr. Frisch, and the thirty-four members of the Mesa Chorus for their gift to us tonight."

Audience applause for those at the back.

"But I also want to acknowledge the appearance of someone invisible -- more than someone -- three, four, perhaps a dozen invisibles whose voices have been haunting the evening. Can you think who they are?"

No answer from the room of thinkers and doers.

"I am referring, of course, to the psalmists and prophets who supplied Mr. Handel with his texts, and us with our spiritual itinerary."

Some mumbling among the crowd. The one comment I clearly caught was, "Now we have to sit through a sermon?" Others seemed intrigued.

Have ye not known? have ye not heard?

Hath it not been told you from the beginning?

Have ye not understood from the foundations of the earth?

It is he that sitteth upon the circle of the earth

And the inhabitants thereof are as grasshoppers..."

The quotation came out of the blue, entirely unprepared by the previous remarks. Furthermore, the Chaplain's voice had taken on a new quality -- or was it the Chaplain's voice at all? The closest approximation was the disembodied voice heard at all hours of the day and night over the Project PA system, but here shorn of its electronic quality. Perhaps it was a practiced ventriloquy used in his denomination. In any case, it seemed to come from the three sides of the balcony rather than from the speaker in front. Gregor, at first joining the audience in the search for the source, was drawn to attention by the characterization of "grasshoppers". After a pause for the exotic voice to dissipate, Chaplain Maple continued.

"Those were the words of First Isaiah, the author of much of Handel's text

Hear, O heavens, and give ear, O earth: I have nourished and brought up children and they have rebelled against me. Thus begins the first and greatest of the books of prophets: a testimony with visionary authority, proud genealogy, cosmic scope -- and an indictment of the rebellious children of the Lord."

A few soldiers stood up to leave, but were signaled back down by imperative sergeants.

"I say 'First Isaiah'. Do all of you know that the 'Isaiah' of the Old Testament is not one, but at least three different people, writing scores of years apart? [Silence.] I hope I am not shocking anyone. These are the words of the First Isaiah, who began to preach in the reign of King Uzziah, in the eighth century BC. First Isaiah was a visionary moralist, calling upon a country in the summit of its power. Uzziah had built the economic resources of Judah as well as its military strength. In Jerusalem there were engines, invented by skillful men, on each of the towers, capable of shooting arrows long distances, and heaving great stones.

But Uzziah's strength had become his weakness. He grew proud, and angry at meddling priests, and as his anger mounted, leprosy broke out on his forehead. *And King Uzziah was a leper to the day of his death, and being a leper, he dwelt in a separate house, for he was excluded from the house of the Lord.*

In the year that King Uzziah died, First Isaiah had a vision: he saw the Lord sitting upon a throne, high and lifted up. Above the throne stood the seraphim, and each one had six wings; and with twain they covered God's face, with twain they covered His feet, and with twain they did fly. Insect-like angels, shielding men from the radiation of God."

Scientists and military brass took wary note. Radiation? The radiation of God? Did the Chaplain know something he shouldn't? Gregor, tachycardic, again noted the insects.

"Those were years of power struggles and shifting strategic alliance. The huge kingdoms of Egypt and Mesopotamia, Babylon and Assyria, alternately triumphed, while tiny Judah played its cards as cleverly as it could, seeking protection without humiliation. First Isaiah lived through the reign of four Judaic kings, and he counseled each to rely not on military protection, but on God. History, he proclaimed, was a stage for God's will and God's work; the rising and falling of willful nations was mere detail.

The West Pointers in the audience struggled to recall their Military History courses.

The louder First Isaiah spoke, the farther he was pushed from centers of power. So he let it be known that politics itself, with its arrogance and disregard of justice, was the problem -- not the solution. And why, Ladies and Gentlemen, and Children of all ages, why is that?

A grand pause. When no answer came the chaplain continued.

Because politics is based on the power of the sword. You know First Isaiah's words: some of you have laughed at them. He announced the day when nations *'shall beat their swords into plowshares and their spears into pruning hooks.'* Are you still listening?   First

Isaiah proclaimed the day when '*nation shall not lift up sword against nation, neither shall they learn war any more.*'

It had become clear that this was to be no short, simple thank-you speech from the religion Division. Some in the audience became restless, some transfixed. The GIs knew they could not leave, and the civilians felt they could not abandon them.

"What were First Isaiah's flight instructions from the Lord?" continued Maple. "Now hear this, friends:

'*Go and say to this people* (this people is you):
Go and say to this people
Hear and hear, but do not understand;
see and see, but do not perceive.
Make the heart of this people fat,
and their ears heavy,
and shut their eyes;
lest they see with their eyes
and hear with their ears,
and turn and be healed.'

What?? What could these instructions mean? Isaiah checked them twice. Prophets are normally charged with making people see and understand; they aim to mobilize their hearts, not put them to sleep. 'How long?' Isaiah asked, appalled. 'How long this tactic?' God's plan was uncomfortably clear:

'*Until the cities be wasted without inhabitant and the houses without man, and the land be utterly desolate.*'

Maple paused to let the thought sink in.

"It is hard to be a prophet," he added. And again that voice from nowhere and from everywhere:

"'*Why is my pain unceasing,*
My wound incurable,

Refusing to be healed?'

Gregor could not believe his ears.

"'I cry by day, but you do not answer:
and by night, but find no rest.
I am a worm, and not human;
scorned by others and despised by the people.'

Why, Isaiah, why? Could it be, my poor Isaiah, that only an outsider, only an exile, can claim the humanity society denies?

Gregor was breathing quickly.

"God's plan was decimation; First Isaiah was assigned to cover the news. Reduce Israel to a remnant, and let things begin again. And the Jews were scattered, and their Temple destroyed.

Pause. Silence. Many Europeans' thoughts shifted course toward Europe.

But in the Exile, a prophet arose who lifted the meaning of the events from mere political history to a cosmic drama of world redemption. This was Second Isaiah, the poet responsible for chapters 40 through 55, for much of the *Messiah* text, a lyrical visionary of the heart. For Christians, Second Isaiah spoke the words that most clearly presage the coming of Christ. The historical, human order is to be overcome by the suffering servant, in Christian thought, the crucified Saviour.

It is not just a few thousand Jewish exiles to whom this prophet speaks, as they sit weeping by the waters of Babylon. Second Isaiah addresses every exile all over the world, every human at a loss to find God, every blind man trying passionately to penetrate the darkness of the future. That, Ladies and Gentlemen, is you.

The root of the problem, indeed the root of all evil, is your false sense of sovereignty, and stemming from it, your pride, your arrogance, your presumption.

'*They worship the work of their own hands,*' the Prophet says, '*that which their own fingers have made. They have chosen their own ways, and their soul delighteth in their abominations.*'

But the Lord is weary of such offerings. Where is contrition? Where is regret?

'*Bring no more vain oblations; your incense is an abomination unto Me.*

When you spread forth your hands,
I will hide My eyes from you;
Even though you make many prayers,
I will not listen.
Your hands are full of blood.'"

Things were becoming truly uncomfortable. This might have gone over in some small southern Baptist church, but this was the Fuller Lodge at Site Y. Chaplain Maple seemed to sense this, and pulled back.

"Let me say a few words about history. This is what the prophets discovered: History is a nightmare. We generally assume that politics, economics and warfare are the substance of history. To the prophets, it is God's judgment of man which is the main issue. They look at history from the point of view of Justice, judging its course not in terms of wealth and success, victory and defeat, but in terms of corruption and righteousness, violence and compassion.

We should not expect the darkness of our history to be dispersed soon by any clever technical or political strategy. We will not receive answers concerning the future because we ask questions of those who cannot

13

know, the vain gods of the nations.

The only solution of the historical problem today lies in the prophetic concept.   Second Isaiah speaks to the exiled remnant of our time, to those in prisons and concentration camps, to those separated from husbands or wives, from children or parents, to those toiling in despair in foreign lands, to those in the hell of modern war. He speaks to every one of us in this room.

How should we respond to his words? Ironically? Dismissively? Angry at their seeming pretentiousness, at the immense gap between the proffered solution and the catastrophic reality in which we live?

Two and a half centuries ago, we opted for *means* to control nature and society. It was a right decision, and we have brought about something new and great in history. But we excluded *ends*. And now the means claim to *be* the ends; our tools have become our masters, and the most powerful of them have become a threat to our very existence.

A century and a half ago, we opted for freedom. It was a right decision; it created something new and great in history. But in that decision we excluded the security without which man cannot live and grow. And now the quest for security splits the whole world with demonic power.

What is the world you are making? Wars, victories, more wars. So many tears. So little regret. And who can sit in judgment when victims' horror turns to hate? What saved Second Isaiah from despair was his messianic vision of man's capacity for repentance.

A Lieutenant Colonel unknown to me walked out. Perhaps he had to relieve himself, but of what was unclear.

Only one thing stands in the way. Do you know what that is? What stands in the way of repentance is the worship of power. Why are human beings so obsequious, so ready to kill and ready to die at the call of kings and chieftains, presidents and generals? It is because we worship might, we venerate those who command might, we are convinced that it is by might that man prevails."

This was heresy to the more uniformed in the crowd.

"The most striking feature of all prophetic polemic is the distrust and denunciation of power in all its forms. You who work here know what I am talking about. The hunger for power knows no end; the appetite grows on what it feeds."

Maple's between-the-lines was growing ominous.

"Now as then, the sword is the pride of man; arsenals, forts, chariots and bombs lend supremacy to nations. War is the climax of human ingenuity, the object of supreme efforts; men slaughtering each other, cities blown to ruins. What is left behind? Agony and desolation. And you think very highly of yourselves, don't you? You *are wise in your own hearts and clever in your own sight.* But into your world, drunk with power, bloated with arrogance, comes Isaiah's word that the swords will be undone, that nations will search, not for gold, power or harlotries, but for God's word.

It seems inconceivable, doesn't it? But to Isaiah it was a certainty: War will be abolished. You shall not learn war any more because you shall seek other knowledge. Your hearts of stone will melt, and hearts of flesh will grow instead. Are you ready for the metamorphosis?"

Richard Feynman got up to leave.

"But wait!" the Chaplain called after him to no avail. "We have forgotten an Isaiah, the Third and last Isaiah, the strangest and most mysterious of the three. In transit from the second, he begins with gentle, female imagery:

'Rejoice ye with Jerusalem, and be glad with her, all ye that love her: rejoice for joy with her, all ye that mourn for her.

That ye may suck, and be satisfied with the breasts of her consolations;

[A titter from the young girls in the audience. Feynman paused at the door.]

As one whom his mother comforteth, so will I comfort you, and ye shall be comforted in Jerusalem.'

Happy ending. Nice and tidy. The American Way. But the Bible is not born of shallowness. [Feynman completed his exit.] I skip to the end of the book and read you the comments of Third Isaiah. After all Flesh has come to worship the Lord, God schedules a little field trip:

'They shall go forth, and look upon the carcasses of the men that have transgressed against Me: for their worm shall not die, neither shall their fire be quenched; and they shall be an abhorring unto all flesh.'

The unending destruction of flesh. The eerie excursion of the chosen to look upon the World's Fair, the abhorrent, endless process of corruption.

'Through the wrath of the Lord is the land darkened, and the people shall be as the fuel of the fire: no man shall spare his brother.

And they shall snatch on the right hand, and be

16

*hungry, and they shall eat on the left hand, and they shall
not be satisfied: they shall eat every man the flesh of his
own arm.*

*Therefore hath the curse devoured the earth, and they
that dwell therein are desolate: therefore the inhabitants of
the earth are burned, and few men left.' So that the Lord
'may do his work, his strange work, and bring to pass his
act, his strange act.'"*

Little Paul Teller started to cry. Mici carried him
out.

"Well may you cry, my young friend. It's a grisly
scandal of a text. The reality of Third Isaiah's judgment
is indeed grim, but it is dishonest to pretend that
reality is otherwise. Where do you in this room fit in
this reality?" With a wave of his arm, he indicated the
entire room. "What's wrong with this picture?"

The tension exceeded the punctured silence before
the final Hallelujah. But there was no Hallelujah --
only the disembodied voice again:

*"'Woe to those who call evil good and good evil,
Who put darkness for light and light for darkness!'
'The stone will cry out from the wall,
Woe to him who builds a town with blood,
And founds a city on iniquity.'*

Chaplin Maple strode quickly from the silenced
room. He was not seen again on site. The dance that
followed had a forced and frantic quality. Gregor
left early to go home to bed. I remained to assay the
effects.

ZARATHUSTRA SPEAKS

Gregor will shortly be committing ritual suicide under the bomb tower. This is his announcement to his friends.

Gregor scheduled his "science party" off the cuff, for the very night we arrived. There were no competing attractions. Klaus Fuchs, Edward Teller, Otto Frisch and I were invited to appear at 11:45 PM (sharp!) at the little blockhouse 50 yards from the W. 10,000 shelter, a building housing one of the three searchlights which were to illuminate the test and its aftermath. A quarter-moon lit the sign on the door: COME IN, SET UP VICTROLA WITH STRAUSS SIDE 3, TAKE YOUR SEATS, TURN ON MUSIC. THANK YOU. Had he gone off his rocker? A happening? A performance piece? In 1945?

I opened the door cautiously, and the four of us filed into the small room. At the eastern end was the big searchlight, staring blankly through a bullet-proof window out into the darkness towards the bomb tower. At the western end was a light brown, regulation army desk, and on it a dark brown Gregor, lying naked on his back, lit only, á la Rite of Spring, by a flashlight hanging from the ceiling, three feet above his abdomen. Between the dark light and the light dark were four folding chairs.

There was something acutely embarrassing about this. I'm sure we all felt it, but I, no doubt, the most, knowing Gregor best. We are not normally embarrassed looking at a "naked" animal. In fact, we rarely think of them as naked. It's not just the hair. Is a butterfly naked? An elephant? One would think Gregor's thick, dark, chitinous cuticle would serve admirably for dress. Not so. There were no exposed genitals or private orifices. Nevertheless. Perhaps it was just his position: supine, legs undulating slightly in the air above him, as it was in the beginning -- so ultimately vulnerable. We took our seats, and just sat there waiting for something, not knowing whether we had come to the right place. But what other place was there?

Eventually, I remembered the box on my lap. I got up, searched in the dark for an electrical outlet, found one on the north wall, and plugged in the Victrola. Edward took the record out of its album and handed it over to me after making sure Side Three was topside. I put the record on the turntable, and said, partly to Gregor, and partly to the attendant God of Oddness, "Do you want the music now?" It sounded so peculiar, a simple human question, subject, verb, object, so out of place in this dark cubicle, out in the midst of this martian, colonized waste land, with that odd object lying on the table. There was no answer; the legs simply kept waving. What could I do but put the arm on the platter?

The room filled with hiss as the needle traversed the empty grooves around the rim. There followed then a sound that seemed as native to the odd occasion as my voice had sounded foreign, a barely perceptible rumble that seemed to come from the rocks under the sand, from the slow magma under the rocks, a long vibration whispering guttural resonance -- perhaps a hymn to the bomb soon to be assembled.

Side 3 of *Also sprach Zarathustra* consists of two sections, *Von der Wissenschaft (sehr langsam),* and *Der*

Genesende (energisch). "On Science" (very slow) and "The Convalescent" (energetic). Science. This was a "Science Party". Science here was a slowly growing fugue, the most "intellectual" of musical constructs, the epitome of Learning, a fugue arising, pianissimo, from the depths of the orchestra, reaching out in a long arch towards ever greater, ear-shattering, triple forte wildness. "Science" here was an all-inclusive structure, a fugue subject containing every chromatic pitch in the octave, in common time, triplets and triplet augmentation -- all in four grave measures. It lumbered from the simple C major of Nature, to the gnarled B major of Man, a half-tone below, like some underground creature afraid to breathe pure air, a grim Alberich, slit-eyed and clench-jawed, forswearing love and plotting revenge. Science.

I remembered well the Nietzsche passage Strauss was addressing, a struggle I found urgently compelling in my undergraduate years. A "conscientious man" asserts that fear is the original and basic feeling-state of mankind, the source of all its virtues, the fount of Science. Fear of wild animals, including the wild animal in oneself, the "inner beast". Such old fear -- refined, spiritualized -- is Science.

Nonsense! cries Zarathustra. Fear is the exception. Courage and adventure, and pleasure in the uncertain -- *that* is mankind's gift. Stealing the virtues of the wildest, most courageous animals: *that* -- refined, spiritualized -- is Science.

As Zarathustra's energy overcomes that of the conscientious man, the music quickens. Gregor, beginning in the same supination he must have awakened to on that horrifying morning during the First War, Gregor, here towards the end of the Second, began to wave his legs in startling, unpredicted patterns, almost as if he were spelling mysterious messages in semaphore, finally generating such torque as to flip him off the desk and on to the floor. So Nietzsche's Convalescent:

One morning Zarathustra jumped up from his resting place like a madman, roared in a terrible voice, and acted as if somebody else were still lying on his resting place who refused to get up. Up, abysmal thought, out of my depth! I am your cock and dawn, sleepy worm. Up! Up! My voice shall yet crow you awake!

German-speaking roosters do not say "Cock-a-doodle-doo". Through some strange linguistic contortion, they tend to cry out "Riki-riki-riki". And that is exactly what Gregor did, screeching and bounding nervously around the room, climbing over the walls and ceiling, over the large search-light, a hair-raising display. The music leapt into completely unexpected flights of fancy, a fantastic dance high in the upper winds, rushing and trilling, while the "Disgust motif" began its feverish appearance until the music, and Zarathustra, and Gregor, all fall down as if dead. After a long pause, seven days in the poem, seven seconds in the score, a rebirth begins which will bring full understanding of their mission on earth -- accompanied by one of the most remarkable passages in the orchestral repertoire, astoundingly light, humorous, Till Eulenspiegel once more, and not Death.

Swish-click, swish-click, swish-click. The automatic changer tried to drop the next side, but none was there; Side 3 was all G had requested. He lay, supine again, diagonally disposed on the floor behind us. I took the needle off the record. We sat there in the grotesque light of a hanging, gently swinging

flashlight and waited, again unsure what to do. After a
pause of perhaps half a minute Gregor, from the floor,
recited *"O Mensch, gib Acht!"*, the tremendous eleven
line poem which occurs next in Nietzsche, though not
in Strauss:

(stroke one)
Oh, man, take care!
(stroke two)
What does deep midnight declare?
(stroke three)
"I was asleep --
(stroke four)
"From a deep dream I woke and swear:
(stroke five)
"The world is deep,
(stroke six)
"Deeper than day had been aware.
(stroke seven)
"Deep is its woe;
(stroke eight)
Joy -- deeper yet than agony:
(stroke nine)
"Woe implores: Go!
(stroke ten)
"But all joy wants eternity --
(stroke eleven)
"Wants deep, wants deep eternity."
(stroke twelve)

For the twelve strokes of midnight, Gregor had
worked with his right lower leg a contraption previous-
ly unnoticed, a hammer hanging upside-down from
a cord slipped over a ceiling beam and fastened high
on the handle. The reader may easily imagine how by

pulling with his toe claws on the latter, the hammer head was caused to strike the metal casing -- which emitted not the expected clack, but a surprisingly full, bell-like tone. In this desert where no clocks chimed, it rang out the apotheosis of midnight.

The final bell having struck, G paused a moment, then jumped up, came around to the front of the chairs, leaned back on the desk like an at-ease lecturer, and addressed us directly:

If we shadows have offended,
Think but this, and all is mended,
That you have but slumbered here
While these visions did appear.
And this weak and idle theme,
No more yielding than a dream:
Man is a bridge, and not a goal,
A rope stretched over the abyss
Betwixt beast and Übermensch.
Goodnight, goodnight,
Parting is such sweet sorrow
That I shall say goodnight till it be morrow.

And he reached up behind him and switched off the flashlight, leaving us all in darkness. After several minutes of sitting in silence, Teller decided G was serious about having said goodnight, and got up to leave. The rest of us followed. As I was about to close the door behind me, Gregor said in a low voice, as if to me alone, "Report me and my cause aright to the unsatisfied." Such was the seed which grew into this telling.